D1044831

TO:

FROM:

DATE:

Published by Christian Art Publishers
PO Box 1599, Vereeniging, 1930, RSA

© 2019
First edition 2019

Designed by Christian Art Publishers

Images used under license from Shutterstock.com

Printed in China

ISBN 978-1-4321-2993-4

20 21 22 23 24 25 26 27 28 29 – 16 15 14 13 12 11 10 9 8

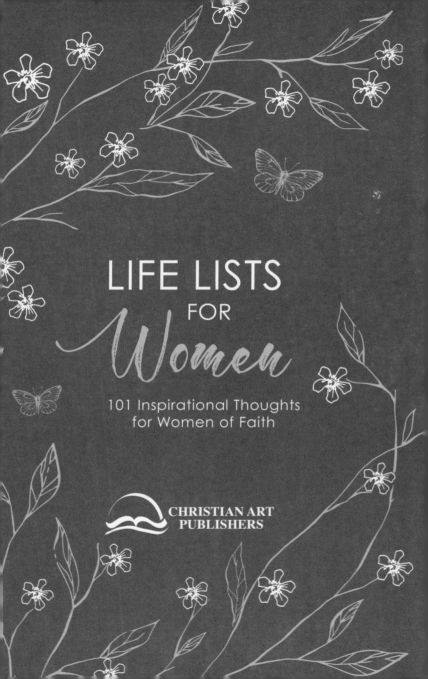

LIFE LISTS

FOR

Women

101 Inspirational Thoughts
for Women of Faith

**CHRISTIAN ART
PUBLISHERS**

Let the morning
bring me word of
Your unfailing love,
for I have put my
TRUST IN YOU.
Show me the way
I should go,
for to You I entrust my life.

Psalm 143:8

1

She
is clothed
with
strength
and
dignity.

Proverbs 31:25

5 REMINDERS
that a godly woman is ...

Wonderfully made

Overjoyed in the Lord

Masterpiece of God

Abundantly blessed

Never alone

GOD BECAME MAN
NOT SIMPLY TO PRODUCE
BETTER PEOPLE OF THE
OLD KIND BUT TO PRODUCE
A NEW KIND OF PEOPLE.

C. S. Lewis

5 Ways to be the best you:

1. Don't copy the behavior and customs of this world, but let God transform you.
ROMANS 12:2

2. If anyone is in Christ, the new creation has come: The old has gone.
2 CORINTHIANS 5:17

3. Put on your new nature, and be renewed as you learn to know your Creator.
COLOSSIANS 3:10

4. Though outwardly we are wasting away, yet inwardly we are being renewed day by day.
2 CORINTHIANS 4:16

5. God gave us new birth and a fresh beginning.
TITUS 3:5

5 RANDOM ACTS OF LOVE

1 } Phone your parents or grandparents just to say hi.

2 } Leave your colleague a note of encouragement.

3 } Volunteer at your church or an animal rescue center.

4 } Make a little extra food for lunch and share it with someone in need.

5 } Take your child for a fun trip to the park.

Do everything in love.

1 Corinthians 16:14

11

Through patience
a ruler can be persuaded,
and a gentle tongue
can break a bone.

Proverbs 25:15

4 REASONS WH'

Better to be patient
than powerful; better to
have self-control than
to conquer a city.

Proverbs 16:32

The end of a matter is better than its beginning, and patience is better than pride.

Ecclesiastes 7:8

PATIENCE IS A VIRTUE

Patient endurance is what you need now, so that you will continue to do God's will. Then you will receive all that He has promised.

Hebrews 10:36

5

LIST 10 THINGS THAT *perfectly* DESCRIBE YOU

1.

2.

3.

4.

5.

6.

7.

8.

9.

10.

You are God's masterpiece.
EPHESIANS 2:10

4 Things you say . . .

[1] There is nothing special about me.

[2] I cannot go one more step.

[3] I cannot take care of myself.

[4] I feel lost and confused.

and what God says to you.

[1]   I have made you special.

[2]   I will carry you.

[3]   I will sustain you.

[4]   I will rescue you.

Isaiah 46:4

FIFTEEN RULES
to simplify your life . . .

1 Start your day with quiet time

6 Clear your work space when finished

4 Declutter daily

2 Prioritize

7 Spend more time in nature

5 No social media 1 hour before and after bed

3 Get a planner

8 Read inspirationa books

Watch less TV

11 Say NO more often

14 Limit the news you watch

12 Avoid negative people

Make a budget and stick to it

15 Focus on what you have, not on what you don't have.

13 Start a hobby

"Be still, and know that I am God."
Psalm 46:10

FIVE THINGS
to remember today

I AM:

1

BLESSED
Ephesians 1:3

2

CHOSEN
Ephesians 1:4

3

ADOPTED

Ephesians 1:5

4

REDEEMED

Ephesians 1:7

5

FORGIVEN

Ephesians 1:7

MY MORE LIST

[1] Get MORE sleep

[2] Drink MORE water

[3] Get MORE exercise

[4] Read MORE

[5] Get MORE organized

[6] Explore MORE

[7] Relax MORE

[8] Have MORE patience

[9] Forget doing "MORE"

[10] MORE of Jesus, less of ME.

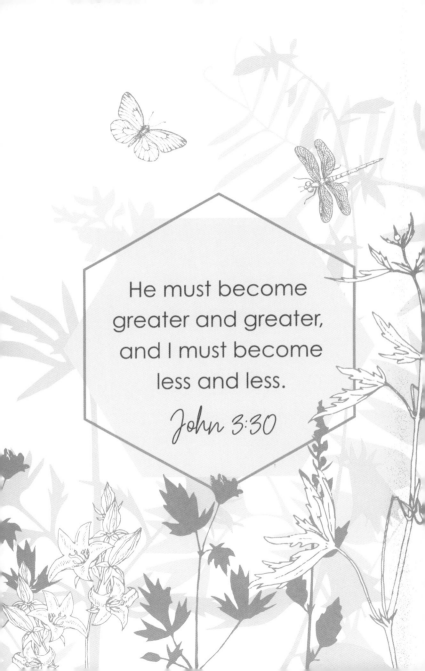

He must become greater and greater, and I must become less and less.

John 3:30

TEACH US
TO NUMBER OUR DAYS,
THAT WE MAY GAIN A
HEART
OF WISDOM.

PSALM 90:12

Make time to:

BAKE A
SURPRISE CAKE

HAVE COFFEE
WITH A FRIEND

WRITE A LETTER

PAINT YOUR DREAMS

SMELL THE FLOWERS

I CAN DO
EVERYTHING
THROUGH
CHRIST,
WHO
GIVES ME
STRENGTH

PHILIPPIANS 4:13

9 Useful Habits

- ~ Make lists
- ~ Carry a notebook
- ~ Quit beating yourself up
- ~ Allow yourself to make mistakes
- ~ Take regular breaks
- ~ Be open to the ideas of others
- ~ Go somewhere new
- ~ Count your blessings
- ~ Take risks

8 MUST-HAVE
WARDROBE ITEMS

SALVATION

Isaiah 61:10

Grace

2 Corinthians
9:13-15

JOY

Psalm 30:11

RIGHTEOUSNESS

Isaiah 32:17

Clothe yourself with ...

PROTECTION

Psalm 5:11

Love

1 John 3:1

Peace

Colossians 3:15

POWER

Luke 24:49

CLOTHE YOURSELF
WITH THE PRESENCE OF THE
LORD JESUS CHRIST.
Romans 13:14

9 POWERFUL PROMISES FOR A PRAYER WARRIOR

1. The eyes of the LORD are on the righteous and His ears are attentive to their prayer.

   1 PETER 3:12

2. "Whatever you ask for in prayer, believe that you have received it, and it will be yours."

   MARK 11:24

3. Pray in the Spirit on all occasions with all kinds of prayers and requests.

   EPHESIANS 6:18

4. "When you pray, go into your room, and pray to your Father. Then your Father will reward you."

   MATTHEW 6:6

5. Build yourselves up in your most holy faith and pray in the Holy Spirit.
JUDE 20

6. Devote yourselves to prayer with an alert mind and a thankful heart.
COLOSSIANS 4:2

7. "Before they call I will answer; while they are still speaking I will hear."
ISAIAH 65:24

8. "If you abide in Me, and My words abide in you, ask whatever you wish, and it will be done for you."
JOHN 15:7

9. When you call, the LORD will answer. "Yes, I am here," He will quickly reply.
ISAIAH 58:9

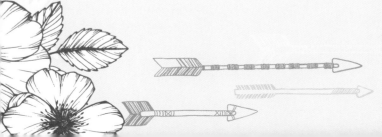

5 PSALMS OF PRAISE AND PROMISE

The LORD is my light and my salvation – whom shall I fear? The LORD is the stronghold of my life – of whom shall I be afraid?

Psalm 27:1

The LORD is compassionate and merciful, slow to get angry and filled with unfailing love.

Psalm 103:8

God is our God
for ever and ever;
He will be our guide
even to the end.

Psalm 48:14

Give thanks to
the LORD, for He is
good; His love
endures forever.

Psalm 118:29

Hope in the LORD!
For with the LORD
there is steadfast love,
and with Him is plentiful
redemption.

Psalm 130:7

PEOPLE WHO *Persevere* DON'T:

EXPECT
FAST RESULTS

DWELL ON
THEIR MISTAKES

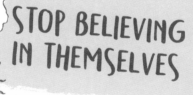

STOP BELIEVING
IN THEMSELVES

STOP
TRUSTING
IN GOD

COMPLAIN MORE
THAN THEY WORK

FOCUS ON
THE PAST

RESIST CHANGE

FEAR WHAT
MIGHT HAPPEN

ASSUME THEIR
PROBLEMS ARE
UNIQUE

SEE FAILURE
AS A SIGN
TO STOP

FEEL SORRY
FOR THEMSELVES

Be strong and do not give up,
for your work will be rewarded.

2 Chronicles 15:7

12 Healthy Habits
TO START TODAY

1. Drink more water.

2. Exercise regularly.

3. Eat a healthy, balanced diet.

4. Spend more time in nature.

5. Set goals and work towards them.

6. Devote more time to doing what you love.

7. Challenge yourself.

8. Smile more.

9. Take time to rest.

10. Go to bed earlier and wake up earlier.

11. Spend more time meditating on God's Word.

12. Set aside time every day to pray.

The LORD will guide you always;
He will satisfy your needs in a sun-scorched
land and will strengthen your frame.

Isaiah 58:11

37

REJOICE ALWAYS,
PRAY CONTINUALLY,
give thanks
IN ALL
CIRCUMSTANCES:
FOR THIS IS
GOD'S WILL FOR YOU
IN CHRIST JESUS.

1 Thessalonians 5:16-18

3 Ways
TO INNER PEACE

1.

Pray and give all your worries and cares to God. Depend on Him and He will help you.

2.

Try to be joyful no matter what happens. Every dark cloud has a silver lining, you just might not be able to see it yet.

3.

Cultivate an attitude of gratitude even when things aren't going as planned.

12 TIPS TO
find calm in the busy

1 Be kind to yourself

4 Do something you enjoy every day

2 Don't compare yourself to others

5 Savor the good moments, and give the bad to God

3 When God has forgiven you, forgive yourself

6 Give yourself enough time to rest and relax

10 Find joy in what you have

7 Cherish your friends and try to make some new ones too

11 Connect more with the people around you

8 Laughter is always the best medicine

12 Focus on what is important to you

9 Do something creative

"Come with Me by yourselves to a quiet place and get some rest."

Mark 6:31

5 STRENGTH-FILLED
promises for today

1 THE LORD GIVES STRENGTH TO HIS PEOPLE; THE LORD BLESSES HIS PEOPLE WITH PEACE.

Psalm 29:11

2 "IN REPENTANCE AND REST IS YOUR SALVATION, IN QUIETNESS AND TRUST IS YOUR STRENGTH."

Isaiah 30:15

3 "I WILL SEARCH FOR MY LOST ONES, AND I WILL BRING THEM SAFELY HOME AGAIN. I WILL BANDAGE THE INJURED AND STRENGTHEN THE WEAK."

Ezekiel 34:16

4 HE GIVES STRENGTH TO THE WEARY AND INCREASES THE POWER OF THE WEAK.

Isaiah 40:29

5 HONOR AND MAJESTY ARE BEFORE HIM; STRENGTH AND GLADNESS ARE IN HIS PLACE.

1 Chronicles 16:27

6 TIPS FOR EARNING RESPECT

[1] Always be kind to everyone.

[2] Treat others the way you want to be treated.

[3] Listen to what others have to say.

[4] Don't make promises you cannot keep.

[5] Don't make excuses, make a plan.

[6] Be open to change and new ideas.

DON'T BE JEALOUS
OR PROUD,
BUT BE HUMBLE AND
CONSIDER OTHERS MORE
IMPORTANT
THAN YOURSELVES.

Philippians 2:3

10 WAYS TO

→ Smile at strangers.

→ Free hugs for friends.

→ Pick up trash even though it isn't yours.

→ Send someone a handwritten note.

→ Put positive sticky notes on your colleagues' computer screens.

Your kindness will reward you.

Proverbs 11:17

sprinkle kindness TODAY

→ Make someone's day with a bunch of flowers.

→ Make coffee or tea for a friend.

→ Hold the door open for someone.

→ Plant a tree.

→ Spend some quality time with the people you love.

10 TIMES WHEN LESS

1. Less social media butterfly

2. Less concrete jungles

3. Less drive-through takeaways

4. Less manic driving

5. Less rat race

6. Less sales receipts

7. Less half-empty glasses

8. Less worry wrinkles

9. Less mouthing off

10. Less binge watching

truly is more...

1. More bookworm

2. More beautiful forests

3. More home-cooked meals

4. More leisurely walks

5. More beach days

6. More crafty DIYs

7. More half-full glasses

8. More smile lines

9. More open ears

10. More Bible studying

Set your minds on things above,
not on earthly things. *Colossians 3:2*

8 VITAL VIRTUES
TO LIVE BY

1. BE CLEAN BOTH INSIDE AND OUT.

2. NEITHER LOOK UP TO THE RICH OR DOWN ON THE POOR.

3. LOSE, IF NEED BE, WITHOUT SQUEALING.

4. WIN WITHOUT BRAGGING.

5. ALWAYS BE CONSIDERATE OF OTHER PEOPLE.

6. BE TOO BRAVE TO LIE.

7. BE TOO GENEROUS TO CHEAT.

8. TAKE YOUR SHARE OF THE WORLD AND LET OTHERS TAKE THEIRS.

Whatever is true, whatever is noble, whatever is right, whatever is pure, whatever is lovely, whatever is admirable – if anything is excellent or praiseworthy – think about such things.

Philippians 4:8

GIVE THANKS TO
THE LORD,
FOR HE IS GOOD!
HIS FAITHFUL LOVE
ENDURES FOREVER.

PSALM 136:1

4 WAYS TO
brighten your day

MAKE SOMEONE SMILE OR LAUGH
SO HARD THEY START TO CRY.

WRITE SOMEONE A THANK-YOU NOTE
TO LET THEM KNOW HOW GRATEFUL YOU ARE
TO HAVE THEM IN YOUR LIFE.

TELL SOMEONE YOU LOVE THEM.

THANK GOD FOR EVERYTHING
HE HAS DONE FOR YOU.

- ❋ Give up worrying about what other people think of you.

- ❋ Give up trying to please everyone.

- ❋ Give up participating in gossip. Speak life.

- ❋ Let go of insecurity!

- ❋ Stop taking everything personally.

- ❋ Give up spending money on what you don't need.

- ❋ Give up anger.

- ❋ Give up control.

FAITH IS CONFIDENCE IN WHAT WE HOPE FOR AND ASSURANCE ABOUT WHAT WE DO NOT SEE.

HEBREWS 11:1

HAPPINESS

Challenge

1 READ AN INSPIRING DEVOTIONAL.

2 SMILE AS MUCH AS POSSIBLE.

LISTEN TO YOUR FAVORITE MUSIC. **3**

BE KIND TO A STRANGER TODAY. **4**

THANK GOD FOR HIS BLESSINGS. **5**

*This is the day that the LORD has made;
let us rejoice and be glad in it.*
PSALM 118:24

May He grant
your heart's desires
and make all your
plans succeed.

Psalm 20:4

5 THINGS TO ACCOMPLISH
in the next year

1.

2.

3.

4.

5.

6 Ways to show
GRATITUDE

1. Give one person the gift of a compliment every day.

2. Acknowledge the little things that make you smile.

3. Be mindful of God's beautiful creation.

4. Donate things you don't use.

5. Write a thank-you note to someone special.

6. Take time to stop and smell the roses.

Give generously

Reciprocate smiles

Acknowledge beauty

Treasure each moment

Inspire happiness

Think positively

Utter life-giving words

Do everything in love

Enjoy God's blessings

29

THE
1 Corinthians 13
WAY TO LOVE

— Be *patient* and *kind* to others.

— *Do not be* jealous, boastful, proud or rude.

— Put *others first* and never demand your own wc

— *Try your best* to not be easily angered.

— *Forgive and forget.* Do not keep a record of the wrong things people have done.

— *Rejoice in the truth* and not in wrongdoing.

— Remember, *love never gives up*, never loses faith, is always hopeful, and endures through every circumstance.

Love is patient, love is kind.
It does not envy, it does not
boast, it is not proud.
It does not dishonor others,
it is not self-seeking,
it is not easily angered,
it keeps no record of wrongs.
Love does not delight in evil but
rejoices with the truth.
It always protects,
always trusts, always hopes,
always perseveres.
Love never fails.

1 Corinthians 13:4-8

12 WAYS TO
stay POSITIVE

1 THINK positively

4 EAT healthy

2 EXERCISE daily

5 WORK hard

3 STAY strong

6 BUILD faith

10 WORRY less

7 PRAY more

11 LOVE always

8 BE happy

12 LIVE fully

9 TRUST God

In Him our hearts rejoice,
for we trust in His holy name.

Psalm 33:21

65

7 STEPS TO

Stop complaining. Instead, practice gratitude and positive thinking.

Change your perspective on negative situations or people.

No more comparing yourself to others. Accept yourself for who you are.

Realize that everyone is human and fallible. So lower your expectations of others and yourself.

contentment

Put God first, people second
and material things never.

Focus on the present rather than
what happened yesterday
or what might happen tomorrow.

Make sure to cherish
the little things in life.

*True godliness with contentment
is itself great wealth.*
1 Timothy 6:6

"*Love* one another. As I have loved *you.*"

John 13:34

Listen
without interrupting.

Speak
without accusing.

Give
without sparing.

Pray
without ceasing.

Answer
without arguing.

Trust
without wavering.

6 KEYS TO A CONFLICT-FREE LIFE

- Be quick to listen, slow to speak.
  JAMES 1:19

- The more talk, the less truth.
  PROVERBS 10:19

- Hatred stirs up conflict, but love covers over all wrong.
  PROVERBS 10:12

- A hot temper causes trouble, patience calms quarrels.
  PROVERBS 15:18

- Kind answers soothe while harsh words stir up anger.
  PROVERBS 15:1

- Treat others the way you wish they'd treat you.
  LUKE 6:31

SMILE ALWAYS
THINK POSITIVELY
GIVE THANKS
LOVE OTHERS
PRAY CONTINUOUSLY
TRUST GOD

8 HOPE-FILLED
promises FOR YOU

1. The LORD is good to those whose hope is in Him, to the one who seeks Him.

Lamentations 3:25

2. Blessed are those whose hope is in the LORD their God.

Psalm 146:5

3. The eyes of the LORD are on those who fear Him, on those whose hope is in His unfailing love.

Psalm 33:18

4. Why, my soul, are you downcast? Put your hope in God, for I will yet praise Him, my Savior and my God.

Psalm 43:5

5. Let us hold unswervingly to the hope we profess, for He who promised is faithful.

Hebrews 10:23

6. Hope will not lead to disappointment. For we know how dearly God loves us.

Romans 5:5

7. Be of good courage, and He shall strengthen your heart, all you who hope in the LORD.

Psalm 31:24

8. We put our hope in the LORD. He is our help and our shield.

Psalm 33:20

35

6 PIECES OF ARMOR FOR A
WARRIOR WOMAN

1.
Belt of truth

2.
Body armor of righteousness

3.
Shoes of the gospel of peace

4.
Shield of faith

5.
Helmet of salvation

6.
Sword of the Spirit

Put on every piece of
God's armor so you will be able
to resist the enemy. Stand your ground,
putting on the belt of truth and the
body armor of God's righteousness.
For shoes, put on the peace that comes
from the Good News so that you will be
fully prepared. In addition to all of these,
hold up the shield of faith to stop the fiery
arrows of the devil. Put on salvation as
your helmet, and take the sword of
the Spirit, which is the word of God.

Ephesians 6:13-17

36

6 Steps

TO LIVING YOUR LIFE WELL

1. GET YOUR PRIORITIES STRAIGHT.

Matthew 6:20-21

2. FILL YOUR LIFE WITH ONLY GOOD THINGS.

Galatians 5:22-23

3. COUNT YOUR COUNTLESS BLESSINGS.

Psalm 107:31

4. LIVE AN ABUNDANT LIFE.

John 10:10

5. FILL YOUR LIFE WITH POSITIVE PEOPLE.

1 Corinthians 15:33

6. PRAY GOD'S WILL.

Matthew 7:7

"Store your treasures in heaven, where moths and rust cannot destroy. Wherever your treasure is, there the desires of your heart will also be."

The fruit of the Spirit is love, joy, peace, forbearance, kindness, goodness, faithfulness, gentleness and self-control.

Give thanks to the Lᴏʀᴅ for His unfailing love and His wonderful deeds for mankind.

"I came that they may have life and have it abundantly."

Do not be misled: "Bad company corrupts good character."

"Ask, and it will be given to you; seek, and you will find; knock, and it will be opened to you."

37

6 GEMS OF Grace

1

God saved you by His grace when you believed. And you can't take credit for this; it is a gift from God.

Ephesians 2:8

2

We are all saved the same way, by the undeserved grace of the Lord Jesus.

Acts 15:11

3

Out of His fullness we have all received grace in place of grace already given.

John 1:16

4

For the grace of God has been revealed, bringing salvation to all people.

Titus 2:11

5

In Him we have redemption through His blood, the forgiveness of sins, in accordance with the riches of God's grace that He lavished on us.

Ephesians 1:7-8

6

You know the generous grace of our Lord Jesus Christ. Though He was rich, yet for your sakes He became poor.

2 Corinthians 8:9

38

Six Promises
FOR YOU

YOU ARE:

1. FORGIVEN

If we confess our sins, He is faithful and just to forgive us our sins and to cleanse us from all unrighteousness.

1 John 1:9

2. FREE

Where the Spirit of the Lord is, there is freedom.

2 Corinthians 3:17

3. GIFTED

In His grace, God has given us different gifts for doing certain things well.

Romans 12:6

4. CHOSEN

"You didn't choose Me. I chose you. I appointed you to go and produce lasting fruit."

John 15:16

5. VALUED

God created human beings in His own image. In the image of God He created them; male and female He created them.

Genesis 1:27

6. BLESSED

Blessed are the people whose God is the LORD!

Psalm 144:15

39

6 ASSURANCES OF GOD'S LOVE

1 He knows your name.

Isaiah 43:1

2 He watches over you.

Psalm 121:5

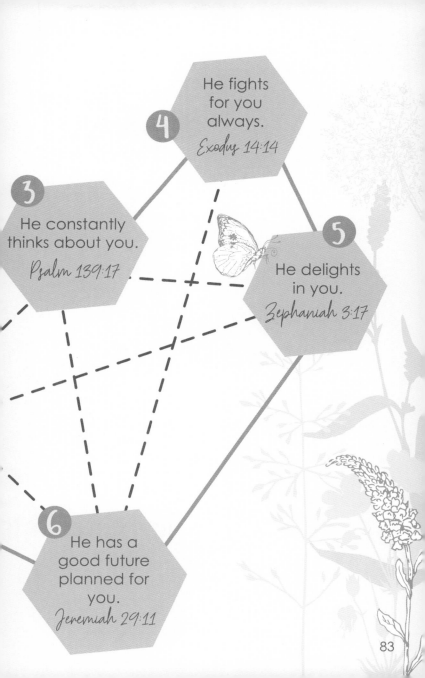

4 He fights for you always. *Exodus 14:14*

3 He constantly thinks about you. *Psalm 139:17*

5 He delights in you. *Zephaniah 3:17*

6 He has a good future planned for you. *Jeremiah 29:11*

40

SPEND TIME
MEDITATING ON
GOD'S WORD.

SIX

BE A PRAYER
WARRIOR.

FIVE

FOUR

BE CONSIDERATE
AND KIND.

MAKE GOD
YOUR FIRST
PRIORITY.

6 TIPS FOR
BEING A
Godly Woman

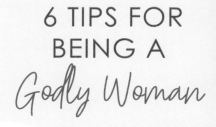

ONE

TWO

THREE

LET GOD'S
LIGHT SHINE
THROUGH YOU.

DO EVERYTHING
IN LOVE.

*Clothe yourselves
with compassion, kindness,
humility, gentleness
and patience.*

COLOSSIANS 3:12

41

5 DAYS TO
AN ATTITUDE OF GRATITUDE

DAY 1   List 5 things you're grateful for today.

DAY 2   The 2 things you value most about yourself are …

DAY 3   List 3 things that made you smile today

DAY 4   Recall a time when God answered your prayer.

DAY 5   Count your blessings

Be thankful in all circumstances, for this is
GOD'S WILL FOR YOU
who belong to Christ Jesus.

1 Thessalonians 5:18

[1] _____
[2] _____
[3] _____
[4] _____
[5] _____

[1] _____
[2] _____

[1] _____
[2] _____
[3] _____

[1] _____
_____

[1] _____
_____

"I have come that they may have life, and have it to the full."

JOHN 10:10

An abundant life.

4 THINGS JESUS

An answer to your

prayers.

"If you believe, you will receive whatever you ask for in prayer."

MATTHEW 21:22

"Everyone who lives in Me and believes in Me will never ever die."

JOHN 11:26

Eternal life with Him in heaven.

PROMISES YOU

You will never be alone.

"I will not leave you as orphans; I will come to you."

JOHN 14:18

43

COMMIT TO
THE
Lord
WHATEVER YOU DO
& HE WILL
ESTABLISH
YOUR PLANS.

PROVERBS 16:3

6 Ways to
TACKLE A TASK

#1 Start off by prioritizing. Organize your to-do list of work according to what is urgent and/or important.

#2 Do not overthink it. Just get stuck in and get it done. Then, move on to the next thing on your list.

#3 Do what you can to limit the distractions around you.

#4 Focus on one task at a time.

#5 Work smarter, not harder. If you are tackling a big task, break it up into smaller pieces and ask someone to help you get it done.

#6 Do your best, but don't try to be perfect.

44

6 Comforting

#1
The LORD comforts His people
and will have compassion on
His afflicted ones.

Isaiah 49:13

#2
"As a mother comforts her child,
so will I comfort you."

Isaiah 66:13

#3
Let Your unfailing love comfort me,
just as You promised me.

Psalm 119:76

ASSURANCES FROM GOD

#4 "I, yes I, am the one who comforts you. So why are you afraid?"

Isaiah 51:12

#5 "Blessed are those who mourn, for they will be comforted."

Matthew 5:4

#6 Praise be to the God and Father of our Lord Jesus Christ, the Father of compassion and the God of all comfort, who comforts us in all our troubles.

2 Corinthians 1:3-4

45

8 FAITH-FILLED
Promises

ONE

"I tell you the truth, if you had faith even as small as a mustard seed, you could say to this mountain, 'Move from here to there,' and it would move. Nothing would be impossible."

Matthew 17:20

TWO

We fix our eyes not on what is seen, but on what is unseen, since what is seen is temporary, but what is unseen is eternal.

2 Corinthians 4:18

THREE

Faith is the substance of things hoped for, the evidence of things not seen.

Hebrews 11:1

FOUR

"Truly I tell you, whoever hears My word and believes Him who sent Me has eternal life and will not be judged but has crossed over from death to life."

John 5:24

FIVE

We live by faith, not by sight.

2 Corinthians 5:7

SIX

When your faith remains strong
through many trials, it will bring you much
praise and glory and honor on the day when
Jesus Christ is revealed to the whole world.

1 Peter 1:7

SEVEN

"Blessed are those who have not
seen and yet have believed."

John 20:29

EIGHT

Because of Christ and our faith in Him,
we can now come boldly and confidently
into God's presence.

Ephesians 3:12

46

Faith's
6-POINT TO-DO LIST

- SPEND TIME WITH GOD.

- MEDITATE ON GOD'S WORD.

- LIVE LIKE THE BIBLE TELLS YOU TO.

- PRAY WITHOUT STOPPING.

- CONFESS YOUR SINS.

- WAIT ON THE LORD.

"Seek the Kingdom of God above all else, and live righteously, and He will give you everything you need."

MATTHEW 6:33

All Scripture is inspired by God and is useful to teach us what is true and to make us realize what is wrong in our lives.

2 TIMOTHY 3:16

Do not merely listen to the word, and so deceive yourselves. Do what it says.

JAMES 1:22

Always pray and never give up.

LUKE 18:1

Whoever conceals their sins does not prosper, but the one who confesses and renounces them finds mercy.

PROVERBS 28:13

Wait for the Lord; be strong and take heart and wait for the Lord.

PSALM 27:14

47

5 WAYS TO
speak life

Let your conversation be always full of grace, seasoned with salt, so that you may know how to answer everyone.
COLOSSIANS 4:6

A wholesome tongue is a tree of life.
PROVERBS 15:4

Let no corrupting talk come out of your mouths, but only such as is good for building up, as fits the occasion, that it may give grace to those who hear.
EPHESIANS 4:29

A gentle answer turns away wrath, but a harsh word stirs up anger.
PROVERBS 15:1

Gracious words are a honeycomb, sweet to the soul and healing to the bones.
PROVERBS 16:24

Think before you speak

T = Is it TRUE?

H = Is it HELPFUL?

I = Is it INSPIRING?

N = Is it NECESSARY?

K = Is it KIND?

5 Blessings
FROM GOD

1

"God blesses those who are humble, for they will inherit the whole earth."

Matthew 5:5

2

"God blesses those who hunger and thirst for justice, for they will be satisfied."

Matthew 5:6

3

"God blesses those who are merciful, for they will be shown mercy."

Matthew 5:7

4

"God blesses those whose hearts are pure, for they will see God."

Matthew 5:8

5

"God blesses those who work for peace, for they will be called the children of God."

Matthew 5:9

49

8 QUESTIONS FOR *self-discovery*

1. When you were a kid, what did you want to be when you grew up?

2. If you could change one thing in your life, what would it be and why?

3. If you could have any super power, what would you choose?

4. What are your spiritual gifts and are you using them to glorify God?

5. If you could jump on a plane tomorrow, where would you go? Why?

6. What makes you smile when you wake up and what do you look forward to?

7. What is your favorite Scripture verse?

8. Is there a person or story in the Bible you strongly relate to? Why?

50

STEP 8

Stop procrastinating and just start.

STEP 7

Focus on one thing at a time and get it done.

STEP 6

Reduce the time you spend on social media.

STEP 5

Set clear deadlines for specific tasks.

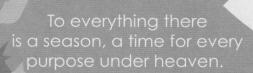

To everything there is a season, a time for every purpose under heaven.

Ecclesiastes 3:1

8 STEPS
TO A
SUPER
PRODUCTIVE
DAY

STEP 1

Don't hit the
snooze button.

STEP 2

Wake up a few
minutes earlier so
you can get more
things done.

STEP 3

Meditate on
God's Word and
pray for God's hand
on your day.

STEP 4

Plan out your
day and make
a to-do list for
yourself.

51

8 STEPS TO *Success*

1 REMAIN OPEN TO NEW IDEAS.

2 LEARN TO EMBRACE CHANGE.

3 MAINTAIN A HUMBLE CONFIDENCE IN YOURSELF.

4 READ GOD'S WORD EVERY DAY.

ALL GLORY TO GOD,
WHO IS ABLE,
THROUGH HIS MIGHTY POWER,
TO ACCOMPLISH INFINITELY
MORE THAN WE
MIGHT ASK OR THINK.

Ephesians 3:20

PRAY WITHOUT CEASING. 5

GIVE EVERY PROJECT YOUR BEST. 6

KEEP A GOOD WORK/LIFE BALANCE. 7

NEVER STOP LEARNING. 8

52

16 ESSENTIALS
for a balanced
LIFE

1. Leave work at work

2. Let go and let God

3. Always tell the truth

4. Listen attentively

5. Think before you speak

6. It's OK to ask for help

7. No is also an answer

8. Declutter your life

Learn from others

14 Be content with what you have

12 Be honest with yourself

Leave the past in the past

15 Don't overdo it

13 Appreciate the little things

Ignore distractions

16 Stop trying to be perfect

YOU MAKE KNOWN TO ME THE PATH OF LIFE;
YOU WILL FILL ME WITH JOY IN YOUR PRESENCE,
WITH ETERNAL PLEASURES AT YOUR RIGHT HAND.

Psalm 16:11

53

6 Blessings
for being
GENEROUS

1. "Give, and you will receive. Your gift will return to you in full – pressed down, shaken together to make room for more, running over, and poured into your lap."

Luke 6:38

2. "Truly I tell you, whatever you did for one of the least of these brothers and sisters of Mine, you did for Me."

Matthew 25:40

3. "When you give to the needy, do not let your left hand know what your right hand is doing. Then your Father, who sees what is done in secret, will reward you."

Matthew 6:3-4

God has a way of giving by the cartloads to those who give away by shovelfuls.

CHARLES SPURGEON

4. Do not neglect to do good and to share what you have, for such sacrifices are pleasing to God.

Hebrews 13:16

5. Whoever is generous to the poor lends to the LORD, and He will repay him for his deed.

Proverbs 19:17

6. A gift opens the way and ushers the giver into the presence of the great.

Proverbs 18:16

54

- Name 4 places you want to visit in your lifetime.
  _ _ _ _ _ _ _ _ _ _

- List 3 things you really want to do before you die.
  _ _ _ _ _ _ _ _ _ _

- If you could only learn one new language before you die, what language would you choose?
  _ _ _ _ _ _ _ _ _ _

- Name a band or musician whose show you still want to see?
  _ _ _ _ _ _ _ _ _ _

- What book do you absolutely have to read while you still can?
  _ _ _ _ _ _ _ _ _ _

- Is there something crazy fun you want to do, but don't feel quite confident enough to pull off, like dying your hair a strange color?
  _ _ _ _ _ _ _ _ _ _

- Who would you like to meet while you still can? Perhaps someone you admire or who inspired you in some way?
  _ _ _ _ _ _ _ _ _ _

- If you could taste one exotic dish, what would it be?
  _ _ _ _ _ _ _ _ _ _

BUCKET LIST

55

5 STEPS
TO REACHING YOUR GOALS

STEP 1

Change the way you think. Set your mind on reaching your goal and start doing what you can to make it happen.

STEP 2

Whenever you take another step towards your goal, celebrate it. Reward yourself for the hard work you've already put in.

Let us run with perseverance the race
marked out for us, fixing our eyes on Jesus,
the pioneer and perfecter of faith.

Hebrews 12:1-2

STEP 3

Do different things on different days
so that you don't get bored before you
even reach your goal.

STEP 4

Keep reminding yourself what your goal
is and why you want to achieve it. This will
keep you motivated to work hard.

STEP 5

Don't expect immediate results.
Rome wasn't built in a day and neither
will you reach your goal immediately.
So stop being so hard on yourself.

56

8 AFFIRMATIONS TO BUILD YOUR *Confidence*

1.
God has made me fearless and strong.

2.
Failures are opportunities to grow.

3.
Nothing is impossible as long as I believe in God.

4.
I make a difference by giving it my all.

5. I am becoming a better version of myself one day at a time.

6. I am blessed beyond measure because God is always with me.

7. Challenges are just another learning experience.

8. I have been created for a marvelous purpose.

Blessed are those who trust in the LORD and have made the LORD their hope and confidence.

Jeremiah 17:7

57

SIX
Reasons not to stress

Jeremiah 29:11

"For I know the plans I have for you,"
declares the LORD, "plans to prosper you and not
to harm you, plans to give you hope and a future."

Matthew 6:26

"Look at the birds of the air: they neither sow nor reap
nor gather into barns, and yet your heavenly Father
feeds them. Are you not of more value than they?"

Hebrews 13:5-6

God has said, "Never will I leave you; never will I forsake
you." So we say with confidence, "The Lord is my helper;
I will not be afraid. What can mere mortals do to me?"

Psalm 55:22

Cast your burden on the Lord, and He shall sustain you;
He shall never permit the righteous to be moved.

Philippians 4:6-7

on't worry about anything; instead, pray about everything.
ell God what you need, and thank Him for all He has done.
Then you will experience God's peace.

Romans 8:28

We know that in all things God works for the good
of those who love Him, who have been called
according to His purpose.

MOMENTS WITH God

In the happy moments,
praise God

In the difficult moments,
seek God

In the quiet moments,
worship God

In the painful moments,
trust God

Every moment,
thank God

DRAW NEAR
TO
God
— AND —
HE WILL
draw near
to you.

James 4:8

6 Blossoms of Beauty
TO GROW IN YOUR LIFE

HONESTY

"Let what you say
be simply 'Yes' or 'No';
anything more than this
comes from evil."

MATTHEW 5:37

HUMILITY

"Whoever wants to be
a leader among you must
be your servant."

MATTHEW 20:26

LOVE

"Your love for one another will prove to
the world that you are My disciples."

JOHN 13:35

MERCY

"Be merciful,
just as your Father is merciful."

LUKE 6:36

OBEDIENCE

"If you abide in
My word, you are My
disciples indeed."

JOHN 8:31

RIGHTEOUSNESS

"The righteous will
shine like the sun in the
kingdom of their Father."

MATTHEW 13:43

GENEROUS

STRONG

WISE

GOD-FEARING

8 TRAITS OF A PROVERBS 31 Woman

NOBLE

TRUSTWORTHY

CARING

DILIGENT

She is clothed with strength and dignity, and she laughs without fear of the future.

Proverbs 31:25

4 WAYS THE *Holy Spirit* HELPS YOU

HE GUIDES YOU

HE TEACHES YOU

HE GIVES YOU POWER

HE HELPS YOU IN YOUR WEAKNESS

"When He, the Spirit of truth, has come,
He will guide you into all truth."

JOHN 16:13

"The Helper, the Holy Spirit,
whom the Father will send in My name,
He will teach you all things."

JOHN 14:26

"You will receive power when the Holy Spirit
comes on you."

ACTS 1:8

The Holy Spirit helps us in our weakness.
For example, we don't know what God wants
us to pray for. But the Holy Spirit prays for us.

ROMANS 8:26-27

A Christian is one whose spirit is led by God's Spirit.

WATCHMAN NEE

62

6 EMERGENCY BIBLE NUMBERS

for when you are ...

ANXIOUS
PSALM 55:22

Cast your cares on the LORD and He
will sustain you; He will never let the
righteous be shaken.

DISCOURAGED
JAMES 1:12

Blessed is the one who perseveres under
trial because, having stood the test, that
person will receive the crown of life.

UPSET
PSALM 147:3

He heals the brokenhearted and
binds up their wounds.

TROUBLED

ISAIAH 43:2

"When you go through deep waters,
I will be with you. When you go through
rivers of difficulty, you will not drown."

LONELY

MATTHEW 28:20

"I am with you always,
even to the end of the age."

SCARED

ISAIAH 41:10

"I will strengthen you and
help you; I will uphold you with My
righteous right hand."

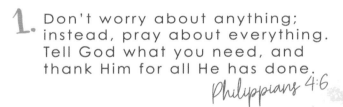

63

5 Scriptures
to have on
SPEED DIAL

1. Don't worry about anything;
instead, pray about everything.
Tell God what you need, and
thank Him for all He has done.
Philippians 4:6

2. Cast all your anxiety on Him
because He cares for you.
1 Peter 5:7

3. "My grace is sufficient for you,
for My strength is made perfect
in weakness."
2 Corinthians 12:9

4. You will keep in perfect peace
those whose minds are steadfast,
because they trust in You.
Isaiah 26:3

5. When anxiety was great within me,
Your consolation brought me joy.
Psalm 94:19

How to deal with
STRESS

SLOW DOWN

TIME MANAGE

RELAX

EXERCISE

SIMPLIFY YOUR LIFE

SPEND TIME IN PRAYER

64

5 REMINDERS OF *God's Love*

"Are not two sparrows sold for a penny? Yet not one of them will fall to the ground outside your Father's care. Don't be afraid; you are worth more than many sparrows."

Matthew 10:29, 31

"God so loved the world that He gave His only begotten Son, that whoever believes in Him should not perish but have everlasting life."

John 3:16

"See, I have engraved you
on the palms of My hands; your
walls are ever before Me."

Isaiah 49:16

"Look at the lilies. They don't work
or make their clothing, yet Solomon
in all his glory was not dressed as
beautifully as they are. And if God
cares so wonderfully for flowers,
He will certainly care for you."

Luke 12:27-28

"Since you were precious in
My sight, you have been honored,
and I have loved you."

Isaiah 43:4

65

LISTEN TO ADVICE
AND
ACCEPT
discipline,
AND AT THE END
you will be
counted among
THE WISE.

Proverbs 19:20

WHAT 5 PIECES OF ADVICE WOULD YOU GIVE YOUR YOUNGER SELF?

1.

2.

3.

4.

5.

66

16 TIPS TO AN
abundant life
& CAREER

1. Challenge yourself
2. Trust God
3. Think outside the box
4. Speak up
5. Know your strengths and weaknesses
6. Set clear goals
7. Respect those around you
8. Be open to new opportunities

Take responsibility for your own actions

14 Do what you love

12 Listen to advice

Invest in yourself

15 Don't procrastinate

13 Show up on time

Never stop learning

16 Know your worth

Whatever you do, do it heartily, as to the Lord and not to men.

COLOSSIANS 3:23

67

Let the Holy Spirit guide
your lives. Then you won't be doing
what your sinful nature craves.

Galatians 5:16

 BIBLICAL TIPS FOR

"Call to Me and I will answer you
and tell you great and unsearchable
things you do not know."

Jeremiah 33:3

If any of you lacks wisdom,
you should ask God, who
gives generously to all without
finding fault, and it will
be given to you.

James 1:5

MAKING GOOD DECISIONS

Who are those who fear
the LORD? He will show them
the path they should choose.

Psalm 25:12

68

THE
10 COMMANDMENTS
for women

1 Always put God first.

2 Worship only God.

3 Revere the name of the Lord.

4 Keep the Sabbath day holy.

5 Honor your father and mother.

Never commit murder.

6

Always be faithful to your spouse.

7

Do not steal.

8

Always tell the truth.

9

Do not be greedy and jealous.

10

"'Love the Lord your God
with all your heart and with all your soul
and with all your mind.'
This is the first and greatest commandment.
And the second is like it:
'Love your neighbor as yourself.'"

Matthew 22:36-40

69

KEEP ON
LOVING
WITH ALL YOUR
HEART.
1 PETER 1:22

5 WAYS TO SAY
"I Love You"

#1 Help your loved one with their chores or work. Doing things you don't like to help them shows just how much you care.

#2 Make a homemade gift. The more effort and thought you put into a gift, the more it will mean to your loved one.

#3 Treat them with breakfast in bed or a home-cooked meal.

#4 Make them a mixed tape. Yes, this is old school, but it can still be just as effective today as it was back then.

#5 Write them a love letter. In today's age of technology and social media, the classics mean so much more than they did before.

70

3 WAYS TO ENSURE YOU ALWAYS DO THE *right thing*

ACT JUSTLY

LOVE MERCY

WALK HUMBLY
WITH GOD

The LORD has told you what is good,
and this is what He requires of you:
to do what is right, to love mercy,
and to walk humbly with your God.

Micah 6:8

Learn to do good. Seek justice. Help the
oppressed. Defend the cause of orphans.
Fight for the rights of widows.

Isaiah 1:17

Let not mercy and truth forsake you;
bind them around your neck, write them
on the tablet of your heart.

Proverbs 3:3

Humble yourselves before the Lord,
and He will lift you up.

James 4:10

4 TIPS
ON HOW TO PRAY

PRAISE and worship God.

REPENT of your sins.

ASK for the needs of others and your own.

YIELD to God's will for your life.

THE PRAYER
OF A
**RIGHTEOUS
PERSON**
IS POWERFUL
AND EFFECTIVE.

JAMES 5:16

6 Reassurances
AFTER AN
OVERWHELMING DAY

1

God will give you rest.

"Come to Me, all of you who are weary and carry heavy burdens, and I will give you rest."

MATTHEW 11:28

2

God is in control.

"Do not fear, for I am with you; do not be dismayed, for I am your God. I will strengthen you and help you; I will uphold you with My righteous right hand."

ISAIAH 41:10

3

God will calm the storm.

Jesus rebuked the wind and said
to the waves, "Silence! Be still!"
Suddenly the wind stopped,
and there was a great calm.

MARK 4:39

4

God has a plan.

"I know the plans I have for you,"
declares the LORD, "plans to prosper
you and not to harm you, plans to
give you hope and a future."

JEREMIAH 29:11

5

God will take care of everything.

Give all your worries and cares to God,
for He cares about you.

1 PETER 5:7

6

God will give you peace.

"Peace I leave with you;
my peace I give you. I do not give
to you as the world gives.
Do not let your hearts be troubled
and do not be afraid."

JOHN 14:27

Remember
THE FRUIT OF THE SPIRIT

LOVE

JOY

FAITHFULNESS

KINDNESS

PEACE

GENTLENESS

FORBEARANCE

GOODNESS

SELF-CONTROL

The fruit of the
SPIRIT
is *Love*
JOY, PEACE,
FORBEARANCE,
kindness, goodness,
faithfulness,
GENTLENESS
AND SELF-CONTROL.

GALATIANS 5:22-23

6 VITAL WAYS GOD
answers you

YOU SAY:

1. "I'm exhausted."

2. "I am unloved."

3. "I don't know what to do."

4. "I'm afraid."

5. "I can't handle this anymore."

6. "I am worthless."

GOD SAYS:

"Wait on Me. I will renew your strength."
ISAIAH 40:31

"I have loved you with an everlasting
love." JEREMIAH 31:3

"I will direct your path." PROVERBS 3:6

"Don't be afraid. I am with you.
I will give you strength." ISAIAH 41:10

"Give your burdens to Me. I will take
care of it." PSALM 55:22

"I have chosen you to be My own
special treasure." DEUTERONOMY 7:6

75

5 Salvation
STEPS TO SHARE

#1 WE HAVE ALL SINNED.

#2 YET JESUS OFFERS US THE FREE GIFT OF ETERNAL LIFE.

#3 GOD HAS SHOWN US HOW MUCH HE LOVES US.

#4 BELIEVE IN JESUS AND YOU WILL BE SAVED.

#5 THOSE WHO ARE SAVED WON'T BE PUNISHED.

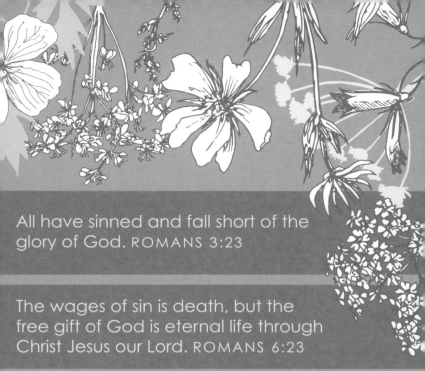

All have sinned and fall short of the glory of God. ROMANS 3:23

The wages of sin is death, but the free gift of God is eternal life through Christ Jesus our Lord. ROMANS 6:23

God demonstrates His own love for us in this: While we were still sinners, Christ died for us. ROMANS 5:8

If you declare with your mouth, "Jesus is Lord," and believe in your heart that God raised Him from the dead, you will be saved. ROMANS 10:9

There is now no condemnation for those who are in Christ Jesus. ROMANS 8:1

76

6 PROMISES
from the
SHEPHERD

#1
God will provide
everything you need.

#2
God will take care
of your soul.

#3
God will protect you.

#4
God will bless you.

#5
God gives you His
goodness and mercy.

#6
God promises you eternal
life with Him in heaven.

The LORD is my shepherd;
I shall not want. He makes me lie
down in green pastures. He leads me
beside still waters. He restores my soul. He
leads me in paths of righteousness for His
name's sake. Even though I walk through
the valley of the shadow of death, I will
fear no evil, for You are with me; Your rod
and Your staff, they comfort me. You
prepare a table before me in the
presence of my enemies; You anoint
my head with oil; my cup overflows.
Surely goodness and mercy shall follow
me all the days of my life, and I shall
dwell in the house of the
LORD forever.

Psalm 23

77

IF YOU WERE STRANDED ON A DESERT ISLAND,

which 5 items would you want with you?

1. _____

2. _____

3. _____

4. _____

5. _____

If I go up to the heavens,
You are there; if I make my bed in
the depths, You are there. If I rise on
the wings of the dawn, if I settle
on the far side of the sea, even
there Your hand will guide me,
Your right hand will hold
me fast.

Psalm 139:8-10

5 ASSURANCES FOR THE *Future*

1
GOD HAS A PLAN FOR YOUR FUTURE.

2
GOD WILL PROSPER YOU AND NOT HARM YOU.

3
GOD WILL GIVE YOU HOPE FOR THE FUTURE.

4 GOD LISTENS TO YOUR PRAYERS.

5 IF YOU SEEK HIS PRESENCE, YOU WILL FIND HIM.

"For I know the plans I have for you,"
declares the LORD, "plans to prosper you
and not to harm you, plans to give you hope
and a future. Then you will call on Me and come
and pray to Me, and I will listen to you. You will
seek Me and find Me when you seek Me with
all your heart. I will be found by you,"
declares the LORD.

Jeremiah 29:11-14

79

6 PROVERBS TO live by

1 THE SEEDS OF GOOD DEEDS BECOME A TREE OF LIFE; A WISE PERSON WINS FRIENDS.

Proverbs 11:30

2 TRUST IN THE LORD WITH ALL YOUR HEART AND LEAN NOT ON YOUR OWN UNDERSTANDING

Proverbs 3:5

3 KEEP YOUR HEART WITH ALL DILIGENCE, FOR OUT OF IT SPRING THE ISSUES OF LIFE.

Proverbs 4:23

WHOEVER GIVES HEED TO INSTRUCTION PROSPERS, AND BLESSED IS THE ONE WHO TRUSTS IN THE LORD.  **4**

Proverbs 16:20

 5 PLANS SUCCEED THROUGH GOOD COUNSEL; DON'T GO TO WAR WITHOUT WISE ADVICE.

Proverbs 20:18

A GENTLE ANSWER TURNS AWAY WRATH, BUT A HARSH WORD STIRS UP ANGER. **6**

Proverbs 15:1

THE PEACE
OF
God,
WHICH TRANSCENDS
ALL UNDERSTANDING,
will guard your
HEARTS
& YOUR
MINDS IN
Christ Jesus.

PHILIPPIANS 4:7

7 Ways to P E A C E

Don't hold on to anger. Forgive others the way God forgives you. **#1**

Stop caring what other people think. God's opinion is the only opinion that matters. **#2**

Happiness is a choice. Choose to be happy today. **#3**

Don't compare yourself to others. God made you unlike anybody else. **#4**

It's OK not to have all the answers. Trust God to give you the answers you need. **#5**

Think before you judge. You might not know the whole story. **#6**

Patience truly is a virtue. God has perfect timing and will give you what you need when you need it. **#7**

165

81

7 AFFIRMATIONS OF *God's guidance*

The LORD will guide you always; He will satisfy your needs and will strengthen your frame.

ISAIAH 58:11

"Call to Me, and I will answer you, and show you great and mighty things, which you do not know."

JEREMIAH 33:3

The LORD directs the steps of the godly. He delights in every detail of their lives. Though they stumble, they will never fall, for the LORD holds them by the hand.

PSALM 37:23-24

Whether you turn to the right or to the left,
your ears will hear a voice behind you, saying,
"This is the way; walk in it."

ISAIAH 30:21

"I will go before you and make the crooked
places straight; I will break in pieces the gates
of bronze and cut the bars of iron."

ISAIAH 45:2

The LORD is good and does
what is right; He shows the proper path
to those who go astray.

PSALM 25:8

The LORD says, "I will guide you along
the best pathway for your life. I will advise
you and watch over you."

PSALM 32:8

82

6 REWARDS FOR A
Humble Heart

1

Humble yourselves
in the sight of the Lord,
and He will lift you up.

JAMES 4:10

2

True humility and fear
of the Lᴏʀᴅ lead to riches,
honor, and long life.

PROVERBS 22:4

3

"I will bless those who have
humble and contrite hearts,
who tremble at My word."

ISAIAH 66:2

"Whoever humbles himself
like this child is the greatest in
the kingdom of heaven."

MATTHEW 18:4

The LORD supports the humble,
but He brings the wicked down
into the dust.

PSALM 147:6

"Blessed are the poor
in spirit, for theirs is the
kingdom of heaven."

MATTHEW 5:3

83

Wise Words
TO LIVE BY

1. "God loves each of us as if there were only one of us."

   St. Augustine

2. When anxiety was great within me, Your consolation brought me joy.

   Psalm 94:19

3. "My grace is sufficient for you, for My strength is made perfect in weakness."

   2 Corinthians 12:9

4. You will keep in perfect peace those whose minds are steadfast, because they trust in You.

   Isaiah 26:3

5. "God never said that the journey would be easy, but He did say that the arrival would be worthwhile."

   Max Lucado

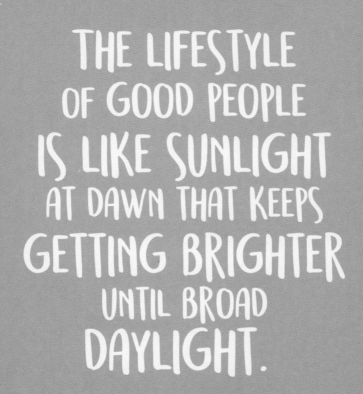

THE LIFESTYLE
OF GOOD PEOPLE
IS LIKE SUNLIGHT
AT DAWN THAT KEEPS
GETTING BRIGHTER
UNTIL BROAD
DAYLIGHT.

PROVERBS 4:18

84

5 SCRIPTURE VERSES
TO HAVE ON YOUR FRIDGE

1

Trust in the Lord with all your heart and lean not on your own understanding; in all your ways submit to Him, and He will make your paths straight.

Proverbs 3:5-6

2

"Be strong and courageous! Do not be afraid or discouraged. For the Lord your God is with you wherever you go."

Joshua 1:9

3

I can
do all things
through Christ
who strengthens me.

Philippians 4:13

4

Set your minds
on things above,
not on earthly things.

Colossians 3:2

5

Whether you
eat or drink,
or whatever you do,
do it all for the
glory of God.

1 Corinthians 10:31

WRITE DOWN 8 THINGS
THAT *inspire creativity* IN YOU

1.

2.

3.

4.

5.

6.

7.

8.

THE LORD HAS DONE
great things FOR US,
and we are filled with joy.
PSALM 126:3

6 THINGS
positive people
DO EVERY DAY

1. Practise gratitude with a gratitude journal.

2. Spend some time enjoying the beauty of God's creation.

3. Eat a deliciously healthy breakfast.

4. Hydrate with some fun fruit-infused water.

5. Listen to really good music.

6. Get enough beauty sleep.

A
CHEERFUL
HEART
is good
MEDICINE.

Proverbs 17:22

87

THE 4 BENEFITS OF HOPING
in the Lord

1. RENEWED STRENGTH.

Being lifted up on wings of
2. FAITH AND HOPE

3. RUNNING THE RACE
of God without growing weary.

4. NEVER FAINTING
with Him by your side.

Those who
HOPE in the LORD
will *renew* their strength.
They will *soar* on wings
LIKE EAGLES;
they will *run* and not
GROW WEARY,
they will *walk* and
not be faint.

Isaiah 40:31

6 Names God
HAS FOR YOU

MY CHILD ------------

BELOVED ------------

**TEMPLE OF
THE HOLY SPIRIT** ------

**CO-HEIR WITH
CHRIST** ------

ADOPTED ------------

AMBASSADOR --------

--

See how very much our Father loves us, for
He calls us His children, and that is what we are!
1 JOHN 3:1

--

As God's chosen people, clothe yourselves with
compassion, kindness, humility, gentleness and patience.
COLOSSIANS 3:12

--

Do you not know that your body is a temple of the Holy
Spirit? You are not your own. So glorify God in your body.
1 CORINTHIANS 6:19-20

--

Since we are His children, we are His heirs. In fact,
together with Christ we are heirs of God's glory.
ROMANS 8:17

--

The Spirit you received brought about your adoption.
And by Him we cry, "Abba, Father."
ROMANS 8:15

--

We are Christ's ambassadors; God is making His
appeal through us.
2 CORINTHIANS 5:20

89

Six Things
ABOUT
FORGIVENESS

ONE

You might not always get an apology, forgive them anyway.

TWO

Try to give people the benefit of the doubt.

THREE

Accept an apology when it's offered without dragging it out.

FOUR

Don't dig up buried offenses.

FIVE

Be the one to extend an olive branch.

SIX

Maintaining good fellowship is
more important than being right.

BE KIND
TO ONE ANOTHER,
TENDERHEARTED,
FORGIVING ONE ANOTHER,
AS GOD IN CHRIST
FORGAVE YOU.

Ephesians 4:32

90

Total
Reliance
Upon
Spiritual
Truths

5 Truths
ABOUT TRUSTING IN GOD

Anyone who trusts in Him
will never be disgraced.

Romans 10:11

1.

Trust in the LORD forever, for the
LORD GOD is an everlasting rock.

Isaiah 26:4

2.

Trust in Him at all times; pour out your
hearts to Him, for God is our refuge.

Psalm 62:8

3.

Those who know Your name trust in You,
for You, LORD, have never forsaken
those who seek You.

Psalm 9:10

4.

The LORD is good, a strong refuge
when trouble comes. He is close
to those who trust in Him.

Nahum 1:7

5.

LIST 5 THINGS
to remember when
you feel *overwhelmed*

1. _____

2. _____

3. _____

4. _____

5. _____

THE NAME
of the
LORD
is a
STRONG FORTRESS;
THE GODLY
run to HIM
& ARE SAFE.

Proverbs 18:10

Six
FEAR-FIGHTING *Truths*

Isaiah 41:13

"I am the LORD your God who takes hold of your right
hand and says to you, 'Do not fear; I will help you.'"

2 Timothy 1:7

God has not given us a spirit of fear and timidity,
but of power, love, and self-discipline.

Psalm 91:4

He will cover you with His feathers. He will shelter you
with His wings.

Psalm 27:1

The LORD is my light and my salvation;
whom shall I fear? The LORD is the strength of
my life; of whom shall I be afraid?

Psalm 121:7

The LORD keeps you from all harm and watches
over your life.

Psalm 118:6

The LORD is on my side; I will not fear.
What can man do to me?

God incarnate is the end of fear;
and the heart that realizes that
He is in the midst will be quiet in
the middle of alarm.

f. B. Meyer

6 KEYS TO LIVING
a great life

#1 GOD FIRST

#2 LOVE ONE ANOTHER

#3 GIVE GENEROUSLY

"DO NOT LAY UP FOR
YOURSELVES TREASURES ON EARTH:
BUT LAY UP FOR YOURSELVES
TREASURES IN HEAVEN."

Matthew 6:19-20

#6 ALWAYS BE KIND

#5 FORGIVE QUICKLY

#4 LIVE SIMPLY

Six
WAYS
God's Word
CAN HELP YOU

Everything that
was written in
the past was written
to teach us.

ROMANS 15:4

3

Your word is
a lamp that gives light
wherever I walk.

PSALM 119:105

2

All Scripture
is inspired by God
and is useful to teach
us what is true and to
make us realize what
is wrong in our lives.

2 TIMOTHY 3:16

1

How can young person stay pure? By obeying Your word.

PSALM 119:9

"Even more blessed are all who hear the word of God and put it into practice."

LUKE 11:28

4

5

Study this Book of Instruction continually. Meditate on it day and night. Only then will you prosper and succeed in all you do.

JOSHUA 1:8

6

Matthew 7:24-25

"Anyone who listens to My teaching and follows it is wise, like a person who builds a house on solid rock. Though the rain comes, it won't collapse because it is built on bedrock."

193

FOUR STEPS
to achievement

1 PLAN PURPOSEFULLY.

2 PREPARE PRAYERFULLY.

3 PROCEED POSITIVELY.

4 PURSUE PERSISTENTLY.

Hard work brings a profit.

PROVERBS 14:23

6 Reminders
that you are
EXTRAORDINARY

1. I praise You because I am fearfully and wonderfully made; Your works are wonderful, I know that full well.

Psalm 139:14

2. You saw me before I was born. Every day of my life was recorded in Your book. Every moment was laid out before a single day had passed.

Psalm 139:16

3. "Before I formed you in the womb I knew you, before you were born I set you apart."

Jeremiah 1:5

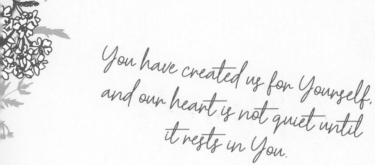

You have created us for Yourself, and our heart is not quiet until it rests in You.

ST. AUGUSTINE

4. God created human beings in His own image. In the image of God He created them; male and female He created them.

Genesis 1:27

5. The Spirit of God has made me; the breath of the Almighty gives me life.

Job 33:4

6. O Lord, You are our Father; we are the clay, and You our potter; and all we are the work of Your hand.

Isaiah 64:8

97

6 Names
OF JESUS

1. THE BREAD OF LIFE

2. THE RESURRECTION AND THE LIFE

3. THE WAY, THE TRUTH AND THE LIFE

4. THE TRUE VINE

5. THE LIGHT OF THE WORLD

6. THE GOOD SHEPHERD

"I am the bread of life; whoever comes to Me shall not hunger, and whoever believes in Me shall never thirst."

John 6:35

"I am the resurrection and the life. The one who believes in Me will live, even though they die."

John 11:25

"I am the way, the truth, and the life. No one can come to the Father except through Me."

John 14:6

"I am the true vine, and My Father is the vinedresser."

John 15:1

"I am the light of the world. Whoever follows Me will never walk in darkness, but will have the light of life."

John 8:12

"I am the good shepherd. The good shepherd lays down his life for the sheep."

John 10:11

98

NAME 6 THINGS
YOU WANT TO BE
Remembered for

1.

2.

3.

4.

5.

6.

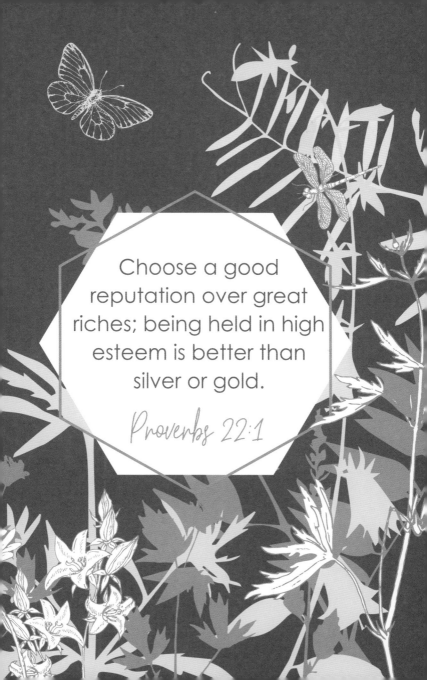

Choose a good reputation over great riches; being held in high esteem is better than silver or gold.

Proverbs 22:1

7 WAYS TO BE
A GOOD *friend*

1. Listen when your friend speaks without interrupting her.

2. Ask her how she is and listen with interest to her response.

3. Encourage and support her in her new endeavors.

4. Help her whenever you can in whichever way she needs.

5. Always be honest and never talk behind her back.

6. Be trustworthy with her secrets.

7. Pray for her.

FRIENDS COME
AND FRIENDS GO,
BUT A TRUE FRIEND
STICKS BY YOU
LIKE FAMILY.

PROVERBS 18:24

100

"I have *come* that they may have *life,* and have it *to the full.*"

JOHN 10:10

10 STEPS TO AN *abundant life*

1. hour of being active

2. liters of water

3. cups of your favorite coffee or tea

4. short mental breaks throughout the day

5. minutes (minimum) of laughter

6. small, healthy meals

7. thousand steps daily, preferably in nature

8. hours of sleep

9. minutes (at least) of Scripture meditation

10. prayers (or more) throughout the day

101

TODAY'S TO-DO LIST:

1 – Pray about everything

2 – Worry about nothing

3 – Praise God lavishly

4 – Criticize sparingly

5 – Give generously

6 – Forgive completely

7 – Love unconditionally

COMMIT TO
THE
Lord
WHATEVER YOU DO,
& HE WILL
establish your
PLANS.

PROVERBS 16:3